S T E V E N   B A K E R

FIRE DANGER

- **Cover Design** : *Evoque Publishing.* ▪

- **Interior Design** : *Evoque Publishing.* ▪

- **Publisher** : *Evoque Publishing.* ▪

- **Editor** : *Daphne Rhea T. Planca.* ▪

First Edition

Printed in London, United Kingdom

Contents

Introduction

Fire.

It has the power to save and to destroy.

It is a gentle ember and a raging inferno.

It is a mate and a monster.

It was fire that catapulted man out of darkness into light. But it has also been an uncontrolled, wild, and unmerciful fire that has raged through our history like a blazing holocaust that has decimated and destroyed.

Today, man has largely tamed fire. We have harnessed it, utilizing its power in a million ways. Yet still the monstrous nature of fire remains. Its deadly power is ever present, and at times it strikes, swift and deadly, leaving carnage in its wake.

When fire strikes, we can feel helpless. Its destructive force is so pervasive; its unremitting advance so lethal that we feel at a loss. So what do we do?

In the face of fire danger, many people place their trust in the authorities-the Fire Department. The United States Fire Department employs over a million full-time professional fire fighters who respond to over 30 million callouts per year. When it comes to urban fire fighting, such as a house fire or a burning vehicle, the Fire Department can usually contain the situation and eliminate the danger.

Wildfires are a different story altogether. A wildfire is a fire that rages out of control like a holocaust of flame that devours everything in its path. In an average year, there are more than 100,000 wildfires across the United States. Wildfires stretch the capacity of the Fire Department to the limit. Men work to a state of utter exhaustion, risking their lives to contain the monster. They do their best, but sometimes the fire wins.

Relying totally on the professional services in the face of wildfire is a mistake. Fire fighters will focus on the concentration of the fire. Yet the fire moves so quickly that they cannot be everywhere all at once.

That leaves homeowners with a choice …

To stand by and helplessly watch as the fire destroys your property, cursing your luck as you contemplate the loss of everything you hold dear,

OR

To work with your neighbors as you out into play a plan that will strategically and systematically defeat the flames.

This book will give you the tools to take control when wildfire threatens your livelihood. It will show you how to prepare, how to work cooperatively with your neighborhood community, and exactly what to do when the fire comes close.

When it morphs into a wildfire, the flames become your enemy. You are at war with that enemy. This book will transform you from being a helpless civilian, about to be consumed as collateral damage, to a frontline soldier, with the power to beat the enemy into submission.

Chapter One

The Two Faces Of Fire

Throughout history, fire has been both mankind's friend and his foe. Without fire, there would be no furnaces, smelters, light, hot water, or heat. We would not be able to cook food or reshape iron. In short, our lives would be radically different if fire had not been discovered by our ancestors 1.9 million years ago.

Fire is not only useful to man but also harnessed by nature. It can rejuvenate a landscape. In fact, fire is an essential part of many forest ecosystems. For thousands of years it has been used as a tool to manage forests. Fire has been used extensively by Native Americans on the Western Prairies and forests to control the mix of animal life, fauna, and flora. As an agent of renewal and change, fire is without equal.

Yet when it gets beyond our control, fire transforms into a

nightmare. Running parallel to the fire-induced advances of mankind, history records the effect of its destructive force.

Fire has been used in warfare for many thousands of years. It is at the basis of all thermal weaponry. The first flame throwers were used by German infantry in the First World War. During the Second World War, firestorms were deliberately created to encircle the cities of Hamburg and Dresden with rings of fire that were being drawn inward by the updraft created by a central cluster of fires.

Nearly every major city in the world has been devastated by fire at some time in its history. Constantinople was devoured by flame five times in 800 years. Some fire disasters stand out in the collective memory Rome in 64 Common Era, London in 1666, and Chicago in 1871.

So just how does this Jekyll and Hyde force of nature work? By understanding the nature of fire, we will be far better equipped to maintain our mastery over it.

The Nature of Fire

Fire is not an object. It is a process-a chemical reaction. The process at play is called oxidation. It is the exact same process that turns the face of a cut apple brown or an iron nail rusty. It happens when oxygen comes in contact with another substance. The only difference between the oxidation of the face of an apple and fire is speed. With fire the oxidation process happens very quickly. In fact, it happens so fast that energy is released. This energy is in the form of heat and light. It causes a rise in temperature and produces smoke.

For a fire to occur, the following three elements, known as the fire triangle, are needed:

▫ Fuel;
▫ Heat;
▫ Air.

We can illustrate this process with a stick and a match. To set the stick on fire, you need to get it to the ignition point, which is around 150°C. This is done by holding the match under the stick. The burning match creates the heat, and once the wood in the stick has reached its ignition temperature, it starts to decompose into chemically volatile gases and charcoal. The volatile gases react with the oxygen present in the air and recombine with the atmosphere to form water, carbon dioxide, carbon monoxide, and other compounds. This process creates heat which starts a chain reaction, bringing any other fuel in the vicinity (the rest of the stick) up to the ignition temperature. The flame that you see is a mixture of volatile gases and solids. It can produce either visible or invisible light.

Methanol burns with an invisible flame. If, however, you set fire to something organic, like a tree, then, thanks to the incandescent soot, it produces that orangey, yellow glow that we call fire. Because the incandescence increases with temperature, we can use the color of flames to give us a rough idea of the temperature of the flames. A barely visible red flame is about 525°C, whereas an orange flame is more like 1200°. A very intense white flame is in excess of 1500°.

Gravity also has a role to play. Because flames are hotter than the air around them and therefore less dense, they will tend to travel upward to an area of less pressure that is why flames have a distinctive pointy shape.

Ground slope plays a critical factor in the fire movement as well. For every 10° increase in incline, the fire doubles its speed. Eighty-kilometer wind will move a fire on a flat ground at 80 km/h within an hour. Increasing the gradient to 10°, this speed becomes 160 km/h.

The fire will continue to burn until one of the three ele-ments-fuel, heat, or air-are removed. Fire fighters can use the fire triangle to fight fires. They can remove oxygen by smothering the fire with a flame retardant, such as a slurry dropped from the air. They can also remove heat by cool-ing the fire with water and fuel by digging a fire line or start-ing a backfire in order to starve the fire of fuel.

Chapter Two

Danger: Wildfire

From our earliest history, fire has been mankind's provider, protector, and destroyer. Over the last 100 years, however, it is in the latter category-that of destruction-that fire has become a curse beyond previous comprehension.

Our TV screens are inundated with images of raging infernos that result from acts of terrorism, arson, and natural disasters. The causes of these types of uncontrolled fires have always been with us. However, we now face them on an unprecedented scale.

Of the manifestations of fire danger, the most terrifying and difficult to control is undoubtedly wildfire. A wildfire is a fire that breaks out in an area of wilderness or countryside, quickly spreading and getting out of control. Wildfires have several distinct characteristics that make them dangerous:

▫ They are quick to change direction.
▫ They are able to spread very quickly.
▫ They have the ability to jump over gaps such as rivers, roads, and even fire breaks.
▫ They can cover a huge area.

Wildfires are classified as "quasi-natural hazards." This means that they may be caused from things other than a natural cause. The five potential ignition sources for wildfires are the following:

1) Human activity;
2) Lightning;
3) Rock fall sparks;
4) Spontaneous combustion;
5) Volcanic eruption.

In terms of human activity, arson is the most common cause. Nondeliberate wildfire ignition is generally the result of neglect, and the most common form of neglect is people throwing cigarette butts out of car windows when traveling through rural areas. Equipment and power line sparks are also contributing factors. The primary cause of wildfire differs around the world. In the United States there are two main culprits—carelessly discarded cigarette butts and sparks from machinery.

The ratio of human caused to naturally occurring wildfires per annum in the United States is 6 to 1. Each year between 7 and 10 million acres are destroyed by wildfire in America.

Some grasses are more flammable than others. Often, when areas of forest are heavily logged, flammable grasses prolif-erate in the area, making it more susceptible to fire.

Spread Of Wildfire

The speed and intensity with which a wildfire spreads are reliant on the fuel that feeds the fire. The type and amount of fuel that is available are largely dependent upon the topography of the landscape. Fire fighters categorize the fuel sources for wildfires as follows:

▫ Subterranean roots fuel ground fires and organic ground material, which burn by smouldering. These types of fire can last for months and are often very difficult to definitively extinguish.

▫ Low-lying vegetation, such as fallen leave and timber, fuels crawling fires, which spread by staying low to the ground.

▫ Midlevel vegetation and tree canopies fuel ladder fires, which scale trees and spread at the canopy level.

▫ Aerial fires are fueled by the tallest trees, vines, and mosses. Not all wildfires will reach the aerial level, depending upon the density of the tree and vegetation life at lower levels.

The less dense a forest is, the easier it is to ignite. This is because the denser a forest is, the more shaded and pro-tected the vegetation and tree life are going to be. This results in lower temperatures and higher humidity. In addi-tion, the less dense potential fuels such as leaves and ferns are, the more easily they will burn. These factors make it more difficult for a fire to ignite in a dense area of bush.

Wildfire Front

Wildfire front is the term applied to the forward moving front part of the fire that meets new, unburned fuel. An approaching wildfire front will prepare any fuel in its path for consumption by heating both the fuel and the air around it. Before the fire even arrives, the surrounding air can reach temperatures in excess of 800°C. In extreme cases, this can cause torching, where fuels such as tree canopies burst forth in flame from below before the main fire even arrives.

Speed

Wildfires can move through dense forest areas extremely rapidly. The rate of movement of a wildfire is known as its Forward Rate of Speed (FROS). The FROS of a bushland fire can be as much as 10.8 km (6.7 miles) per hour. For a grassland fire, the FORS has been known to reach 22 km (14.6 miles) in an hour.

Not all wildfires advance in a forward moving pattern. The fire may form on a tangent to the main fire, forming a flanking secondary fire. Sometimes, a backfire will form which burns in the opposite direction to the main fire.

Fires are able to cross barriers such as roads, rivers, and man-made fire breaks due to the actions of the wind, which can blow hot embers or other burning materials across the gap.

Large wild fires can have a significant impact on the surrounding atmosphere. As it is heated, air rises, causing a strong updraft that pulls in cooler air from the surrounding atmosphere. The result can be a tornado-like whirl of hot air that can move at speeds of up to 80 km per hour (50 mph).

Increased U.S. Danger

Over the last decade, the Western United States has seen an increase in both the scale and frequency of wildfires. As climate changes associated with El Niño continue to cause temperatures to rise and droughts to become more wide-spread, the risks are only going to increase.

Between 1984 and 2001, the region between Nebraska and California saw an average increase of seven fires per year that destroyed more than 1000 acres of land. During that same period, more than 4000 homes have been destroyed by wildfire. Yet, from 2001 to 2014, the average number of houses destroyed per year has more than tripled to 1354.

A 2014 study in Geophysical Research Letters, a journal produced by the American Geophysical Union, published these results, along with their analysis of what has led to the unprecedented increase. They found that in nearly all cases where there was a marked increase in wildfire activity, there was correspondingly severe drought activity. The researchers concluded that large-scale climate changes are a major contributing factor in the wildfire increase.

The coauthor of the study, Max Moritz, said, "Most of these trends show strong correlations with drought related conditions which, to a large degree, agree with what we expect from climate change projections."

It is interesting to note that the study posited that successful wildfire suppression over previous decades may have also contributed to the recent upsurge.

"It could be that our past fire suppression has caught up with us, and an increased area burned is a response of more continuous fuel sources," as the coauthor Jeremy Little said. "It could also be a response to changes in climate, or both."

The study identified the following regions of the Western United States as the areas with the greatest increase in wild-fires:

- Rocky Mountains;
- Sierra-Nevada Mountains;
- Arizona-New Mexico Mountains;
- California (southwest desert);
- Nevada;
- Arizona;
- New Mexico;
- Texas;
- Southern Plains (Texas, Oklahoma, Kansas, and eastern Colorado).

Wildfires and Houses

Homes that are in the path of a wildfire are most likely to catch fire as a result of embers and firebrands. Firebrands are objects that have caught alight and are carried by the wind. Sometimes these burning missiles can travel a mile before depositing themselves. If a firebrand lands on a roof, it can very quickly ignite leaves or needles.

Surface fires can also lead the fire into a home, especially if highly flammable grasses and shrubs are leading up the pathway. Radiant heat from causes such as closely situated tree tops that quickly spread canopy fire can cause a type of spontaneous combustion inside a house well before the actual flames get anywhere near it.

Chapter Three

Taking Control

The United States Fire Department does a stellar job at keeping the nation fire safe. The service employs more than 1.1 million fire fighters, of whom about 400,000 are career fire fighters. When a wildfire strikes, however, the resources of the service is stretched to its limits.

Fighting wildfires is a dangerous and an exhausting work. Over the past decade, an excess of 200 fire fighters has died while fighting wildfires. Heat stress and fatigue are the two biggest risk factors.

Over recent years, there has been a marked increase in the number of people who are choosing to live in rural areas on the edge of forest lands or on remote mountain sites. They often relocate for the more relaxed lifestyle and enjoy the breath taking panorama. But they also take on the very real challenge of facing a wildfire.

Wildfires often start without anyone noticing. It is not until they are well under way that they come to attention. Then they spread rapidly, bringing fear and anxiety with them. Amidst the panic and chaos, those who are prepared are the ones who will come off the best.

When it comes to protecting yourself, your family, and your worldly possessions from wildfire, you have simply got to take ownership. You cannot leave it all to the Fire Department. It is up to you to take control.

The first thing you need to do is to assess your current wildfire risk level.

The Wildfire Zone

Federal authorities have determined a zoning system for people who live in rural wildfire areas. People who live within two miles of a natural forest area of woodland (including forests, native grasslands, shrubs, wetlands, and clear-cuts) are classified as living with the Wildland Urban Interface Zone (WUI). Within that zone is the Ember Zone. Those who live within a mile of a natural area are in the Ember Zone.

Of the 48 contiguous states in the United States, 19 of them have more than 50 per cent of their homes in the WUI. California has more than 5 million homes within the WUI. To assess your individual level of wildfire risk, check out the following resource:

www.southernforests.org

Within the WUI, there are three grades of fire hazard:

Low Hazard:

▫ Short grasses;
▫ Low growing shrubs and plants;
▫ Mainly deciduous trees;
▫ Noncontiguous greenbelts;
▫ Lots of firebreaks (roads, pools, and paveways);
▫ Humid climate.

Medium Hazard:

▫ Abundant wildlands;
▫ Tall, heavy grasses;
▫ Small, flammable shrubs;
▫ Dry, windy climate;
▫ Predictable dry season.

High Hazard:

▫ Dense forest;
▫ Highly flammable vegetation;
▫ Unbroken canopy;
▫ Abundance of tall shrubs;
▫ Dry season lasts more than 3 months.

It is sobering to realize that more than 65 per cent of homes in the combined U.S. WUI zone are in high-hazard areas. In addition, more than 80 per cent of WUI zone land has not yet been built upon. That means that there is an ever increasing potential for wildfire catastrophe as new rural building projects proceed in the coming years.

Your Wildfire Action Plan

Those who take the time to foresee the potential calamity and have in place a well-rehearsed, cogent plan of action are far more likely to minimize the impact of a wildfire. When the fire threatens, it is only natural that your anxiety level will rise. Having thought through just what you need to have at your disposal and what actions each member of the family should take will greatly reduce your stress, making it far more likely that you will respond in a way that will heighten your chances of getting out safely.

Your plan of action needs to be with a simple checklist to speed up the access to emergency services as follows:

▫ Post emergency telephone numbers along side every phone;
▫ Ensure that the entrance to your driveway from the mailbox is clearly indicated;
▫ Make sure that your house number is clearly labelled on your mail box.

Around the home you need to make sure that the equipment that you needed will be available where you can reach it quickly.

You need to have a small water source within close proximity. This could be a small pond, a swimming pool, a cistern, or a water reservoir. You also need to ensure that you have several well-maintained hoses of adequate length to make it to the outer reaches of your property.

Make sure that you have the following well-maintained items within easy reach:

▫ A rake;
▫ An axe;
▫ A handsaw;
▫ A chainsaw;
▫ A bucket;
▫ A shovel.

Plan to have two means of exit from your property and ensure that all drivers are familiar with them. It is quite likely that the main exit route will be blocked.

Discuss with the members of your family a place to meet that is outside of the community in case you get separated. You should also make arrangements with a family member or friend who is outside of the community to be your contact person in case local phone lines are down. This person can also act as a single point of contact for family members. Rather than trying to cross communicate over heavily burdened phone and internet lines, a third party who is outside the danger zone can coordinate communications more effectively.

If you and other family members will be leaving the area in two or more vehicles, you need to have two-way radios in order to stay in contact. Do not rely on your cell phone to communicate. Smoke will interfere with your cell phone reception.

The Go Bag

A go bag is an easily transportable, lightweight bag that contains all of the essential items that you will need if you are required to evacuate in a hurry. It is essential that you have a go bag prepared and within easy reach. Here is what it should contain:

▫ Your most important documents in a waterproof holder;
▫ Spare keys for your vehicles and residence;
▫ Money including financial cards;
▫ Three days' worth of food;
▫ A flashlight, radio, your phone (do not forget spare batteries);
▫ Any medications that are needed by family members;

▫ A well-equipped first aid kit;
▫ Wet weather clothing;
▫ Three days' supply of water;
▫ Area Map;
▫ Swiss Army Knife or similar multipurpose tool.

You need to get hold of a heavy-duty duffle bag as your Go Bag. Make sure that you load the heaviest items at the bottom of the bag. Put clothes in resealable zip-lock bags. Keep your Go Bag stored year round in an easily accessible location.

It may be that you would not have access to your home and simply have to jump in the car and go. For that reason, you should have a second go bag already sitting in the car ready to go.

You should also ensure that you always have a sturdy pair of shoes and a flashlight within reach if you have to suddenly evacuate during the hours of darkness.

Your "If Time Allows" List

Every wildfire situation is different. One situation may require that you simply grab hold of your "Go Bag" and get the hell out of there. Another may allow you a little time—maybe 30 min-to gather up some essentials that will give you a head start if you have to start rebuilding your life. If you have not thought about it, that 30 min can be a mind-boggling panic fest that leaves you grabbing for the nearest thing in sight. Having a prethought-out list of essentials, however, can make your start over a lot less painful.

Think of the things that you are always using. Here are some common essentials that you will probably want to have on your list:

▫ Cell phones and chargers;
▫ Computers, external hard drives, and power cords;
▫ Purses and wallets;
▫ Important documents such as birth certificates, marriage certificates, passports, insurance papers and contact information, tax files, school, and medical records;
▫ House plans;
▫ Passwords for online accounts;
▫ List of service providers and their contact numbers.

To determine what irreplaceable special items should also be on this list, you should hold a family meeting. Ask each family member to close their eyes and imagine that they have just lost everything in the home. Now have them open their eyes and look around. What thing(s) would they be absolutely devastated to lose? For most people this will be an object that has more sentimental than economic value. Once you identify each person's special item, add it to your list.

What About the Animals?

When you evacuate you will obviously be taking your pets with you. But what if the temporary accommodation that you move into does not allow for pets? Your local Humane Society should be able to help you with temporary care of your small pets. To make this process easy, make sure that you are up to date with any inoculations and registration for your pets.

If you run livestock, you may well have to rely on their natural survival instincts in the event of a wildfire. You should check out where you are able to evacuate your stock to. Have a ready supply of food and water at this new location. If you have not got a big enough trailer to fit all of your animals into, you should simply leave all of your gates open. Do not plan on making multiple trips in and out of the area.

Wildfire Action Plan Checklist

✔ A designated meeting place for all the family outside of the danger zone;

✔ A number of exit routes from the home and the area;

✔ An evacuation plan for animals and pets;

✔ An out-of-area contact who can act as c single point of contact for all family members;
Fire extinguishers that should be working and family members know how to use them;

✔ All family members that should know how to turn off gas, electric, and water mains;

✔ A portable radio or scanner that will allcw you to keep up-to-date with the progress of the fire.

Chapter Four

Fire Proofing Your Property

So you are one of the millions of homeowners who live in the WUI high fire hazard zone. What can you do to your property to make it as fire ready as possible? This chapter will step you through five key steps that you can take to greatly improve your chances.

Step No. 1: The Fire-Resistant Roof

Your roof is the most fire vulnerable part of your house. A wooden or shingle roof is the worst type of covering; it can turn your home into an instant tinder box. Shingle roofing can be especially dangerous as the shingles are likely to dislodge and become burning missiles that fly across the landscape, potentially starting spot fires. The most fire-resistant roofing material is composition, metal or clay or terracotta tile. In fact, shake shingles are now illegal in wildland areas in some states. If you have a wooden or shingle roof, you should consider reroofing. This is an expensive exercise but will make your home a lot safer. In addition, it is more than likely that your insurance costs come down quite substantially when you inform your insurer that you have replaced your roof with fire-resistant materials.

Areas between roof coverings should be covered to prevent fire embers catching on them. Roof and crawl space vents can also cause problems. It is not hard for moisture to get trapped in these areas, with resultant mold growth. In addition to these areas, the following types of vents are potential hot spots for embers to alight:

• Inlet and outlet vents in attics;
• Soffit vents;
• Through roof vents;
• Gable-end vents;
• Ridge vents.

Embers can rain down on roofs for hours, both before, during, and after a wildfire. Vents are the roof's weak spots. Make sure that yours are cleaned, covered, and clear of bristles and other debris.

The edge of your roof can be especially problematic.Wherever the angle of the roof changes, such as when it meets a wall, it is likely that debris will build up. This is the same place where embers will accumulate in the event of a wildfire. That is why it is critical that you regularly maintain your gutters and other areas where the angle of the roof changes.

Clay tile barrel roof covering can also be a big problem. Wind-borne debris can easily become trapped in these tunnel areas, making them prime fuel sources for flying embers. A cut to shape metal strip can be placed over these ends to be covered.

Step No. 2: Windows

Windows that face vegetation are the most liable to fire breakage. Often single pane windows shatter before the fire gets close, providing an airway and space for rapid entry. For that reason, the number of windows that face areas of vegetation should be limited. Double glazed or tempered windows not only make your home more energy efficient but also provide an extra level of protection in case of fire. Window and door screens should be made of metal as opposed to plastic or timber. All decks, eaves, and vents should have a metal skirting around them to prevent embers from pushing through.

If the window frame ignites, the frame can burn through other exterior materials as well as igniting items, such as curtains, inside the home.

Step No 3: The Deck

Your deck space can be especially problematic during a wildfire. Decks are categorized by the type of deck covering, of which there are two main types:

▫ Deck board floor covering;
▫ Solid surface floor covering.

Deck board floor coverings invariably use combustible materials such as timber. Solid surface floor coverings are usually made from noncombustible materials such as concrete or tile. Open frame decks are often susceptible to build up of debris on their underside and between the decking boards. Make sure to regularly clean between board gaps.

Step 4: Defensible Space

Defensible space is the legally required gap between your property and the surrounding wildland area. Defensible space is the first and most practical line of defense between your home and a fire. Adequate defensible space can slow or even halt the advance of the flames. It also provides clearance space for fire fighters to defend your property.

The Fourmile Canyon Wildfire in 2010 brought home the importance of having adequate defensible space. The official report on the disaster concluded that lack of defensible space was the main reason for the loss of the 474 homes that were destroyed in the blaze.

Defensible space is more than just another piece of bureaucratic red tape to make your life miserable. It is an absolutely vital factor in saving your home—and your life.

The required amount of defensible space differs from state to state. In California, it is 100 feet. This means that you need a clear space of 100 feet all the way around your home. That does not mean, though, that the area has to be a barren wasteland.

Landscape your property with wildfire safety uppermost in your mind and you can create an appealing yard that is also fire safe. The smart use of driveways, water features, paths, and decking areas can create that wow factor without compromising your safety.

The following Fire Service suggestions will ensure that you have an effective defensible zone:

▫ Have nothing at all that is flammable within 5 feet of your house.

▫ Within 5–30 feet of the house, use low-growing plants that are spaced well apart. Do not allow any tree branches to overhang the house. If you plant trees (hardwood are best) in this zone, trim the branches 10 feet from the ground. Make sure that there is, at least, a 30 foot gap between crowns.
▫ Keep the lawn well watered.
▫ Within 30–100 feet of the house, use low-growing plants.
▫ Add in such fire breaks as walkways, rock gardens, water features and paved driveways.
▫ Within 100–200 feet, thin out and create space between trees. Do not allow the crowns of tall trees to touch.

Step 5: Landscape Maintenance

Regular maintenance of your property is essential in reducing your fire risk. You need to keep well on top of the following:

▫ Mowing;
▫ Pruning;
▫ Weeding;
▫ Removing dead vegetation.

Regular maintenance of your property is especially important if the house is a holiday home, which is the case for about 25 per cent of all properties in the WUI. You need to make sure that someone is regularly doing your maintenance. If you do not, you will turn what is probably your biggest investment into a potential death trap.

Chapter Five

Essential Fire-Fighting Equipment

Having the rights tools for the job ccn often make the differ-ence between success and failure. When it comes to some-thing as serious as fighting wildfire you have absolutely no room for leeway-you simply must hcve the right equipment. In this chapter, we will review the essential hand tools and power tools to allow you to effectively and safely prepare for and combat a fire.

Hand Tools

You do not need to purchase expensive power tools in order to get your property fire safe. As well as saving on air pollution, hand tools allow you to get some exercise while you spruce up your property.

Pruning Saw

A simple, folding pruning saw is the most important tool in your possession. Having it in your pocket as a matter, of course, will allow you to trim branches whenever you spot them.

There are a variety of models available. Your best value for money is the Silky Pocket Boy 170, which retails for about $40.

Hatchet

A hatchet is a multipurpose tool that is compact and affordable. It can be used for limbing trees or as a hammer to bang in wedges when felling a tree.

Ax

A good chopping ax offers a viable alternative to a chainsaw for those who only have a few trees to cut. An ax has a longer handle length than a hatchet, along with a sharper blade.

For chopping wood, a chopping ax has a handle that is too short to do the job safely. For splitting wood, you need a proper splitting saw with a 36 inch handle and a wedge-shaped head.

Machete

To sort through a lot of bush, you need a good bush machete. Do not buy a Chinese one—it will not be durable enough. Rather, look for a machete that is made in Central or South America. It should have a thin, high-carbon steel blade with a length of 26 or 28 inches.

Machetes come from the manufacturer only partially sharpened, so you will need to get hold of c good sharpening stone.

Swing Blade

A swing blade is a great tool for cutting dry grass. It comes in a variety of forms, from a lightweight, L-shaped variety to a triangular frame weed cutter and a long-bladed scythe. The grass whip style allows for ease of handling and provides a long pendulum swing.

Winch and Pulley

A winch and pulley apparatus is an indispensable tool if you have to cut down a tree which is leaning in the wrong direction. It is also great for pulling out stumps. Make sure that you place the pulley high in the tree in order to redirect the rope and make dragging easier.

Lopper

Loppers allow you to chop off small limbs on high trees or reach into dense brush. A lopper is a long-handled pruner that you can pick up for around $25. As well as pruning, this tool can also act as a long-handled hammer to knock off dead branches.

Pole Saw

A pole saw is a more robust tool than a lopper, allowing you to more effectively cut into distant limbs. A 12 foot pole saw will allow you to get to most canopy branches that require trimming.

A good pole saw accessory is a hook that will allow you to pull branches downward.

Rake

A good rake is essential to keep your defensible zone safe. Leaves, pine needles, and pine cones need to be cleared regularly, and you need the right tool to do it effectively.

There are actually five types of rake:

- Leaf;
- Shrub;
- Bow;
- Thatch;
- Fire.

For a sturdy enough tool to work with pine needles and cones, you should opt for a rake with steel tines. Also having a fire rake is a smart move, as it will contain four-tempered triangular teeth and is lightweight.

McLeod Tool

The McLeod tool is a combination of a hoe, a rake, and a tamper. This makes an incredibly versatile tool that is capable of cutting, loosening, and moving vegetation and soil.

Pulaski Tool

Invented by Ed Pulaski as he battled the 1910 Big Burn, this tool is a hybrid between an ax and an adze. It can chop like an ax while also cutting through roots and ploughing up the hard earth.

Pickeroon

The pickeroon looks like an ax but has a sharpened pointed blade at the business end. This makes it ideal for dragging timber without having to bend and reach, thus saving your spine.

Power Tools

Chainsaw

A chainsaw is a fantastic labor-saving device. But it is also a tool that can cause serious injury, even death. Ensuring that you follow basic safety rules is essential. A chainsaw is only a dangerous tool if used improperly. The chain travels at around 75 miles per hour, and you would not have time to get out of the way if it kicks back.

That is why most saws have a kickback feature, which will stop the blade in the event of a kickback. You should ensure that your blade is extremely sharp. If the blade is dull, it will cut at an angle; it will dig and grab and go in a direction that you do not want. If you do not know how to sharpen a saw, take it to somebody who is qualified to do the job properly.

When you are making your cut, rather than standing on top of the blade, stand a little to the side. This precaution will mean that it would not kick back directly into your face if it kicks back. You should also keep both hands on the saw at all times. Always make your cuts at 90° to the log.

Follow the manufacturer's recommendation on getting the chainsaw started. Make sure that it is well accelerated before making contact with the tree so that it will cut straight away. If you try to ease into the tree, it will grab and throw the saw in an attempt to kick back.

Your saw will probably have a series of large teeth that are positioned vertically at the base of the blade. This allows you to dig the teeth into the tree while you are cutting. This provides a surface to let the chainsaw do the work.

The most important consideration when choosing a chainsaw is the length of the bar. The length of the bar will determine the size of tree you can cut. Bars in the 12–14 inch range are best suited for light yard work. For a more powerful, versatile machine, go for a bar in the 16–20 inch range. Anything with a bar over 20 inches is going to be very heavy and very powerful.

The other significant consideration when purchasing a chainsaw is the type of power source. There are three options:

- Electric;
- Battery operated;
- Gas powered.

Electric chainsaws tie you to a power source, which will be way too limiting for your needs. The major drawback with battery-powered saws is that you would not find one with a bar length in excess of 16 inches. For your needs, then, a gas-powered saw is going to be the best option for wildfire safety work.

String Trimmer

A string trimmer will make taking care of long grass a whole lot easier. String trimmers also come in electric-, battery-, and gas-powered varieties. Electric trimmers work best if you are working within 200 feet of your power source. Battery-powered trimmers do not usually stack up in the power stakes when you are faced with a challenging job. For major clearing jobs, a gas-powered trimmer makes the most sense.

Wood Chipper

A wood chipper allows you to turn a potential fire hazard

into fine mulch ready for composting. You will want one that has a large enough funnel to cope with branches that are up to 3 inches thick. You will want at least a 5 horse power gas-powered motor. A good wood chipper will set you back close to $1000. You may find it a better option to hire a chipper from your local hire center.

Chapter Six

You and Your Neighbors: Strength in Numbers

We live in a world where neighbors are virtual strangers. The camaraderie of past generations is nowhere to be seen as people go about their lives in isolation, neither wanting nor needing to engage with those who live around them.

For you though, it is different. The very fact of where you live ties you to your neighbors in a way that just does not apply to urbanites. You and your neighbors together face the daily risk of fire sweeping through your community and destroying everything. And, even though your nearest neighbor may be miles away, you need to work together to ensure that you all come through.

That is the where the Firewise Communities Program from the National Fire Protection Association (NFPA) comes into play. The Firewise Communities Program teaches homeowners and WUI community members how to decrease the risk of losing their homes while best protecting themselves in the event of a fire. The Program draws on community spirit in conjunction with their willingness to reduce wildlife risk and ecosystem balance.

By becoming a Firewise community, you will greatly improve your community's relationship with your local fire staff. It also encourages cooperation and support among neighbors, paving the way for a seamless joint effort when the pressure comes on. Neighbors can help neighbors better than anyone else; after all, you are inextricably linked in your wildlife safety solutions.

The following five steps are required for a community to become a part of the Firewise program:

1) Create a community wildfire risk assessment in conjunction with the local fire department or a state forestry agency.

2) Form a board and generate an action plan from the community wildfire assessment.

3) Hold an annual Firewise Day Event

4) Invest a minimum of $2.00 per capita per annum in local fire safety initiatives.

5) Submitting an application and annual report to your local Firewise liaison.

The Community Meeting

The first step to becoming a Firewise community is to call a community meeting. The following suggestions will help you to put together a presentation. You may elect to do this in the form of a Powerpoint presentation, or as a straight talk:

▫ Introduce the concept of the role of wildland fire. Stress that fire is natural and essential but that it can also put homes at risk.

▫ Know the community and its needs-reassure people that becoming a Firewise community does not mean that the authorities are going to come in and "uglify" their property. Show them examples of beautifully landscaped defensible space.

▫ Use specific examples, citing wildland areas of high risk.

▫ Use plain language and avoid jargon.

Talking in front of a group can be quite daunting for many of us. What do we say? How do we get our points across in a convincing way? To make this process as stress less as possible, we here provide a sample script that you can use when speaking in front of your community:

Sample Script

Hi, I am _____. I really appreciate your taking the time to come together as a community to discuss an important issue that affects each of us, wildfire.

Wildfire is a natural, ongoing process. Its incidence is becoming more frequent and more families are losing their property and having their lives endangered.

By the simple act of living in our area, we take responsibility for being proactive in fighting wildfire.

In our own area, wildfire is also occurring more regularly.

We can expect to encounter a wildfire every XX years.

Right now, this year, our biggest risk factor is *(INSERT DETAILS, E.G., DROUGHT; DRY SEASON; FUELS; BUILD-UP. Be specific about types of fuels in the area.)*

▫ **We cannot expect the fire service to protect our property. The fire may physical prevent them from doing so, and their resources may just be too stretched.**

▫ **That does not mean that our homes are at the mercy of the flames. We as a community need to step up and take control of our own destiny. We have the power together to prepare our families and our property in order to get through.**

In order to reduce the negative outcomes cf a wildfire event, we need to do things differently. We need to make modifications to our development, building, and landscaping practices.

People who live and recreate in fire-prone lands assume a certain level of risk and responsibility due to the condition of the surrounding environment.

Understanding the Enemy

In order to be fully prepared to face a wildfire, we first need to learn about how wildfires proliferate. The three key elements that impact upon the spread of fire are the following:

• Fuels;
• Weather;
• Terrain;

Dry and windy weather conditions will allow a wildfire to

quickly spread. Low humidity and drought will result inextremely dry vegetation, making it far more likely to ignite.The level of wind can make the difference between a small, contained fire and a raging inferno. Powerful winds can also transport firebrands across large areas, sparking off new aspects of the fire.

The terrain of the landscape also affects the rate at which the fire advances. Fire moves more slowly up hill, and fires that go up a grade have longer flames. The reason for this is that the fire "preheats" all of the vegetation that is above it and its path. Two other factors that affect the rate of the fire are slope and sunlight. South-facing slopes have more exposure to sunlight, resulting in much dryer vegetation.

For our community to effectively prepare and fight a wildfire, we need to establish partnerships with:

• Federal and State Agencies;
• Tribal Governments;
• Fire Service;
• Agencies.

• Local Federal and State Agencies have the responsibility to lower the wildfire risk on public land. For them to do that effectively, we need to be working with them on our private land. Of course, they do not have the right to tell us what to do on our own land, but we need to be proactive in fire safing our property. One way we can do this is by creating a Firewise Community. The Firewise Community program will allow us all to live compatibly with fire, safe in the knowledge that we have the knowledge and ability to work effectively together.

• The National Firewise Communities program is an interagency program designed to encourage local solutions for safety in the wildland/urban interface by involving home owners, community leaders, planners,developers, firefight-ersers, and others in the effort to protect people and property from the risk of wildland fire.

• The vision of Firewise Communities is: With adequate planning and cooperation among varying interests, wildfires can occur without disastrous loss of life, property, and resources.

• Research tells us that if we really want to reduce our risk of the wildfire threat to our homes, we need to focus right in our own backyards. We need to focus on the home and its immediate surroundings.

• Federal and state land managers are taking care of the public lands, but it is our responsibility to reduce the hazards on our private property.

• Landscaping is among the first elements of a home that others notice. If managed effectively, landscaping can also serve as a fuel break, protecting a home in the event of a wildfire.

• The primary goal for Firewise landscaping is fuel reduction-limiting the level of flammable vegetation and materials surrounding the home and increasing the moisture content of remaining vegetation.

• Firewise landscaping also allows plants and gardens to reveal their natural beauty by leaving space between individual and groups of plants and trees.

• Even if a landscape is designed in perfect compliance with Firewise recommendations, fire may still reach your home.

• Remember that heavy winds can carry firebrands over the tops of trees to land on a roof. If that were to happen to your home, your home's exterior must play an important role in preventing ignitions that could lead to total home destruction.

• Keep in mind that the home ignition zone **includes the home**, in relation to its immediate surroundings within 100 to 200 feet.

• When considering improvements to reduce wildfire vulnerability, the key is to consider the home as part of the entire home ignition zone—the house itself and its immediate surroundings within 100 to 200 feet.

▫ The home's vulnerability depends on how much flammable vegetation and other hazards are surrounding it, in relation to the vulnerability of the home's construction materials.

▫ The higher the fire intensities within the home ignition zone, and the greater the firebrand exposure from the wildfire, the more you need nonflammable construction materials and a resistant building design.

▫ In other words, if you want to have trees and vegetation close to your home, you need to use building materials that are less likely to burn and vice versa.

• In addition to preparing your home and family for potential wildfires, consider working with your neighbors to prepare your entire neighborhood.

▫ When a residential community has taken proactive measures to prepare homes to survive a wildfire, the fire service is able to focus more of its resources on the main body of the fire as opposed to individual structures.

• In cooperation with state forestry organizations, Firewise Communities has developed a nationwide program to recognize communities that maintain an appropriate level of fire readiness-Firewise Communities/USA.

▫ This program is of special interest to small communities and neighborhood associations that are willing to mitigate against wildfire by adopting and implementing programs tailored to their needs.

▫ The communities create these programs themselves with cooperative assistance from state forestry agencies and local fire staff.

• If this community is interested, I can arrange for a forestry representative to help begin the assessmen⁻ process for this community.

• The reality today is that fire agencies cannot solve the problem alone.

▫ Fire fighters do not have the resources to defend every home during a wildfire. Personal responsibility is the key.

▫ Residents can take steps to reduce their risks. We know that using Firewise strategies can increase the likelihood of our homes surviving a wildlcnd fire threat.

• There are no guarantees that our communities will be fireproof—some fires just get too big and too hot. But if we take action to be firewise, we greatly increase the chances that our homes and communities will withstand a wildfire.

(Sample script courtesy of the National Fire Protection Association - http://firewise.org/wildfire-preparedness/public-service-announcements.aspx)

Gaining Firewise Community Registration

In order for your community to become a Firewise Community group, the following steps need to be taken:

1) Contact Firewise-complete and online request form at www.firewise.org/usa.

2) Visit by Firewise liaison to assess the WUI zone area.

3) Create a community "spark plug" consisting of home owners and fire professionals who will comprise your local Firewise board and work on your Firewise Community plan.

4) Assessment and Evaluation-the Firewise liaison will present his report to the board.

5) Creating a Plan-the board creates a plan that focuses on the recommendations in the Firewise liaison report.

6) Implement local solutions following the schedule designed by the board.

7) Apply for recognition-to achieve Firewise Community recognition status, you must submit your application form along with a Firewise Community Plan and Firewise event documentation to your community liaison.

Firewise Action Day

The required annual Firewise Action Day is an excellent opportunity for neighbors to build community spirit while working with their local fire professionals. Of course, it will also greatly enhance your community's fire readiness.

A "Chipper Day" is an excellent idea for your annual event.

It involves community members coming together to conduct fire mitigation work involving trimming and chipping overgrown areas of public and private land. The local fire service often provides a free chipper for the day to facilitate removal of waste vegetation. An alternative activity would be to create fire breaks in strategic locations as identified on the Community Action Plan.

Firewise Action Days usually begin early in the morning and work until midafternoon, when a community potluck lunch is held. It is good to involve as many people as possible to make the event inclusive. As an example, moms and younger children could distribute safety brochures to homes while men and teenage boys work on hazard reduction activities.

The Neighborhood Pod

A neighborhood pod is a group of six to eight adjacent households who work together to meet the wildfire challenge. If one of the homeowners is away when the fire strikes, the others will look after their own homes first, then work together to protect the home of the family who are not there.

Arrange regular get-togethers with the members of your pod. Have a potluck or a barbecue, preceded by a meeting that covers each other's special requirements. Do not rely on neighbors, as they will be primarily focused on their own needs. By talking about your children, pets, elderly relatives, or other considerations, however, you will be enabling them to assist as they can.

At pod meetings talk about what fire mitigation work has been done, sharing examples of effective work. You should also plan what work homeowners will undertake in the coming months and schedule the next meeting 6 months ahead.

Set up an emergency phone tree, where neighbors each call three other people to get vital information out quickly. An initiator makes the first three calls. After all calls have been made, the person at the bottom of the list calls back the initiator to confirm that he has got the message. The emergency phone tree should be tested regularly to ensure that it works.

Chapter Seven

Secret Synergy: Interlocking Arcs of Water

To be able to withstand the ferocity of an approaching wild-fire, it is imperative that neighbors stand together, working in unison to harmonize their attempts to halt its advance. Of course, if the fire is raging out of control and you have been advised to evacuate, then you need get the hell out of there. The idea of homeowner's standing their ground reso-lutely in the face of overpowering flames and fumes is the stuff of nightmares for fire fighters. The best advice is to get out and to get out early. So long as you have followed the preparatory advice already given-especially regarding the minimum amount of defensible space-then you have got a good chance of coming out with your home still intact.

There are times, however, when it may be safer to stay where you are. According to Fire Management Consultant Bob Mutch, "It's incredibly dangerous on the road if you've waited too long." Mutch says, "Power lines are down, there's smoke and embers everywhere. You can't see. People drive off the side of the road, or into a tree, and they die. It's tragic."

Mutch advises leaving, but with a provision.

By leaving early, we mean, really early, way before an evacuation," says Mutch, whose Painted Rocks Fire District in Montana is one of the few in the nation to espouse this model. "But if you know what you're doing, you're prepared, you've created your defensible space and you're mentally ready, then you should be allowed to defend your home."

An advantage of staying on site is that you are able to douse smouldering embers that remain after the fire has passed through. It is often these very embers that end up destroying homes in the wake of wildfire.

If you are going to stay, however, you had better know what you are doing. You need to have fire-resistant clothes (such as Nomex), a steady water supply, and a pump.

From the Combat Zone

As we have emphasized throughout this publication, fire is your enemy. In learning to combat it, it is appropriate, then, that we look to the military. It is from the combat zone that we find the concept of interlocking arcs of fire.

Interlocking arcs of fire, or crossfire, refer to the sighting of automatic weapons, such as machine guns, so that their arcs of fire overlap. The tactic became widespread during World War One and is a means of providing mutual support for a brother in arms. By providing a continuous arc of fire in all directions, it is very difficult for an attacker to find a cover approach to a defensible position. This was an especially useful tactic when it came to trench warfare. Machine gun clusters, or nests, would protect the front of the trench. The crossfire would be set up across No Man's Land, with the result that many lives were lost. The fire would never be directed to the direct front but to the flank.

Fighting a fire will be a little different, but the concept remains the same. Fire can be considered a living being. People often describe a moving fire "as if was alive." In order to combat this living entity, neighbors need to work together in a similar manner as two machine gunners pouring interlocking arcs off ire upon their enemy. We refer to this concept as

Interlocking Arcs of Water

The main fire front is attacked by the householder who is in its direct path, while the householder on either side uses the interlocking arcs concept to pour water onto the flanks of the blaze. This concentration of water from three fronts is an extremely effective way of making use of the limited water supply. Once the front is either extinguished or controlled, the neighbors can switch to the new threat, moving with the fire but still pouring water into it from directly in front as well as from both flanks. This will bring water from a minimum of two points onto any one point of fire.

For the interlocking arc of water concept to work, it is essential that each home have its own independent water supply. You will not be able to rely on the city's water supply as that will very quickly dry up in the emergency, leaving you with little more than a dribble coming from your hose. You might consider having a well with a pump installed or a bore hole drilled. Storage tanks should have a 500 gallon water capacity.

There are also systems available that create a curtain of water around a house to help stop ember attack. Ember attack is the most likely cause of a house fire and can actually start sometime (hours or even days) after the fire has passed.

It is highly likely that installing your own independent water supply will significantly reduce the cost of your home insurance.

Chapter Eight

Your Wildfire Essential Checklist

Wildfire does not have to be your master. By working together with your community, you are able to make, not just your property but also your entire community, a safer place.

Here is a recap on what you need to do before, during, and after wildfire strikes.

Before a Wildfire

✔ Develop a wildfire action plan;

✔ Prepare a Go Bag;

✔ Have an "If Time Allows" list;

✔ Make a plan to evacuate animals;

✔ Fire proof your property, with a focus on roof, windows, and deck;

✔ Clear leaves and debris from eaves, gutters, and porches;

✔ Ensure that you have a minimum of 100 feet of defensible space;

✔ Regularly maintain your landscape;

✔ Make sure that you have well-maintained essential fire fighting equipment and know how to use it;

✔ Initiate your community's involvement in the Firewise Communities Program.

During a Wildfire

✔ Remain attuned to the latest news on the movement of the fire and community announcements;

✔ Put your Go Bag in your car;

✔ Place patio or deck furniture inside;

✔ Close off all gaps where embers may collect such as vents, windows, gabled roof ends, and eaves;

✔ Connect garden hoses and fill tubs, pools, and water containers;

✔ When you are told to evacuate, get out fast;

✔ If the decision is to stay and defend, work with your neighbors to use the interlocking arcs of water method to combat the fire.

After a Wildfire

✔ Keep listening to news updates;

✔ Examine your property. First, do a quick inspection to make sure that nothing is burning. Then get a rough damage estimate.

✔ Contact your insurance company to go over claims.

To receive free updates on further releases from Steven and

other material related to Fire danger from Evoque Publishing

sign up at the following Url: www.evoquepublishing.com/signup

www.ingramcontent.com/pod-product-compliance
Lightning Source LLC
Chambersburg PA
CBHW040313010626
45792CB00022B/284